The Monarchy in Britain

LONDON HER MAJESTY'S STATIONERY OFFICE

Prepared by

Reference Division

Central Office of Information, London
©Crown copyright 1981
First published 1974
Fourth edition 1981

354·42
CEN
113399

ISBN 0 11 701026 X √

0107783

N.B.—This pamphlet is one of a series produced by the Central Office of Information for British Information Services. To meet requests from inquirers in the United Kingdom, certain pamphlets in the series are being made available on sale from Her Majesty's Stationery Office.

Contents

Introduction

Since the Queen came to the throne in 1952 her reign has seen the British monarchy adapt to major changes in Britain's position in the world and in British society. A large proportion of the dependencies over which she reigned on her accession have become independent members of the Commonwealth, of which she is Head, and many of whose members continue to recognise her as head of State. Modern communications enable the Queen and the royal family to make more overseas visits than ever before. In Britain, television has brought them much closer to the people, and meetings with ordinary men and women at home and abroad have accelerated the trend towards making the British monarchy a less aloof institution, while still evoking the national memory of centuries of history. The Queen personifies both national and Commonwealth unity, and the entire royal family play a supporting role, undertaking arduous programmes. A combination of the formal and the informal is a special feature of today's monarchy, combining traditional pomp and ceremony with direct contact with people from all walks of life in their towns or at work. Both in Britain and during Commonwealth tours, 'walkabouts'—mingling with the crowds—have become a popular feature. Royal jubilees, birthdays and weddings provide opportunities for a practical affirmation of the close and affectionate relationship between the monarchy and the people.

The development of the monarchy during the Queen's reign is only the most recent example of its long evolution in the light of changing circumstances. It is the oldest secular institution in Britain, going back to at least the ninth century. The Queen can trace her descent from King Egbert, who united all England under his sovereignty in 829. The monarchy antedates Parliament by four centuries, and the law courts by three. Its continuity has been broken only once (during the republic under Cromwell from 1649 to 1660).

There have been interruptions in the direct line of succession, but the hereditary principle has always been preserved. In Anglo-Saxon times the 'Kings of the English' were elected by the *Witan* from among the males of the royal line, and the elective principle was, in form at least, preserved under the first Norman kings, who submitted themselves to election, or more accurately 'recognition', by the *Commune Concilium* (an act of recognition still forms part of the modern coronation service). Thereafter the hereditary system became firmly established.

For centuries the monarch personally exercised supreme executive, legislative and judicial power, but with the growth of Parliament and the courts, the direct exercise of these functions gradually decreased. The seventeenth-century struggle between Crown and Parliament led, in 1688–89, to the establishment of a limited constitutional monarchy. The monarch, however, remained the centre of executive power throughout most of the eighteenth century, and appointed and dismissed ministers. By the end of the nineteenth century, with the establishment of responsible government and of the modern party system, the monarch's active participation in politics had become minimal.

Responsible government in Britain has two main elements: ministers are responsible to Parliament in that they cannot govern without the support of an elected majority; and they are responsible for the advice they tender to the Queen, and, therefore, for any action she may take. Political decisions are taken by the ministers, and the Queen is left free to perform the functions of an impartial head of State.

This pamphlet describes the monarchy as it operates today and some of the traditions associated with it.

The Royal Family

QUEEN VICTORIA 1819–1901
m. Prince Albert of Saxe-Coburg and Gotha (Prince Consort)

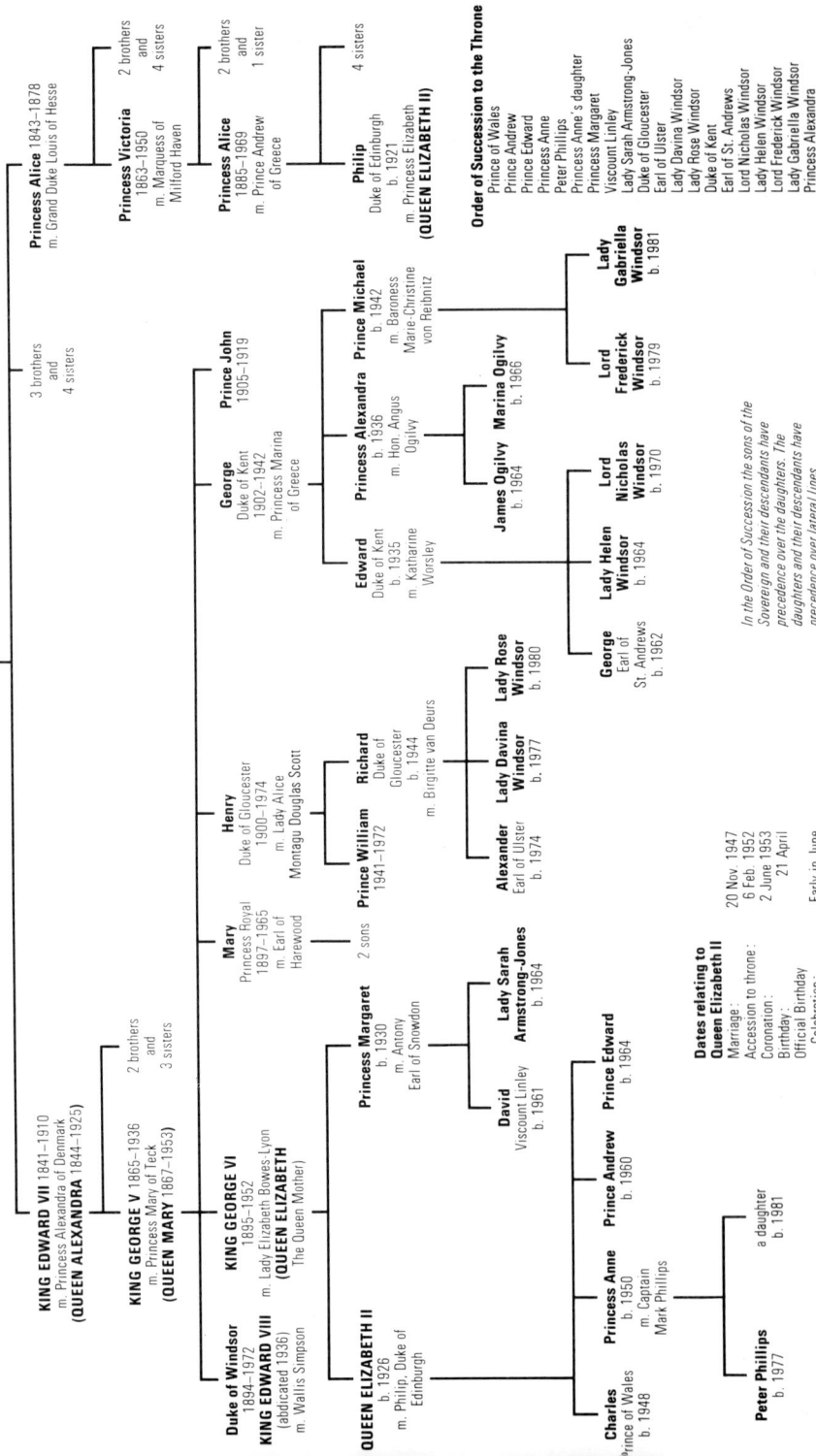

3 brothers and 4 sisters

Princess Alice 1843–1878
m. Grand Duke Louis of Hesse

2 brothers and 4 sisters

Princess Victoria 1863–1950
m. Marquess of Milford Haven

2 brothers and 1 sister

Princess Alice 1885–1969
m. Prince Andrew of Greece

4 sisters

Philip Duke of Edinburgh b. 1921
m. Princess Elizabeth **(QUEEN ELIZABETH II)**

Order of Succession to the Throne
Prince of Wales
Prince Andrew
Prince Edward
Princess Anne
Peter Phillips
Princess Anne's daughter
Princess Margaret
Viscount Linley
Lady Sarah Armstrong-Jones
Duke of Gloucester
Earl of Ulster
Lady Davina Windsor
Lady Rose Windsor
Duke of Kent
Earl of St. Andrews
Lord Nicholas Windsor
Lady Helen Windsor
Lord Frederick Windsor
Lady Gabriella Windsor
Princess Alexandra

In the Order of Succession the sons of the Sovereign and their descendants have precedence over the daughters. The daughters and their descendants have precedence over lateral lines.

KING EDWARD VII 1841–1910
m. Princess Alexandra of Denmark **(QUEEN ALEXANDRA 1844–1925)**

KING GEORGE V 1865–1936
m. Princess Mary of Teck **(QUEEN MARY 1867–1953)**

2 brothers and 3 sisters

Duke of Windsor 1894–1972 **KING EDWARD VIII** (abdicated 1936) m. Wallis Simpson

KING GEORGE VI 1895–1952
m. Lady Elizabeth Bowes Lyon **(QUEEN ELIZABETH** The Queen Mother)

QUEEN ELIZABETH II b. 1926
m. Philip, Duke of Edinburgh

Mary Princess Royal 1897–1965 m. Earl of Harewood
2 sons

Henry Duke of Gloucester 1900–1974 m. Lady Alice Montagu Douglas Scott
Prince William 1941–1972
Richard Duke of Gloucester b. 1944 m. Birgitte van Deurs
Alexander Earl of Ulster b. 1974
Lady Davina Windsor b. 1977
Lady Rose Windsor b. 1980

George Duke of Kent 1902–1942 m. Princess Marina of Greece
Prince John 1905–1919
Edward Duke of Kent b. 1935 m. Katharine Worsley
George Earl of St. Andrews b. 1962
Lord Nicholas Windsor b. 1970
Lady Helen Windsor b. 1964
Princess Alexandra b. 1936 m. Hon. Angus Ogilvy
James Ogilvy b. 1964
Marina Ogilvy b. 1966
Prince Michael b. 1942 m. Baroness Marie-Christine von Reibnitz
Lord Frederick Windsor b. 1979
Lady Gabriella Windsor b. 1981

Princess Margaret b. 1930 m. Antony Earl of Snowdon
David Viscount Linley b. 1961
Lady Sarah Armstrong-Jones b. 1964

Charles Prince of Wales b. 1948
Princess Anne b. 1950 m. Captain Mark Phillips
Peter Phillips b. 1977
a daughter b. 1981
Prince Andrew b. 1960
Prince Edward b. 1964

Dates relating to Queen Elizabeth II

Marriage:	20 Nov 1947
Accession to throne:	6 Feb. 1952
Coronation:	2 June 1953
Birthday:	21 April
Official Birthday Celebration:	Early in June

The Royal Family

When the Queen was born on 21 April 1926, her grandfather, King George V, was on the throne and her uncle was his heir. She was the first child of the Duke and Duchess of York, and was christened in the chapel of Buckingham Palace, being given the names Elizabeth Alexandra Mary. The death of her grandfather and the abdication of her uncle (King Edward VIII) brought her father to the throne as King George VI and she became heiress presumptive. As a child her studies were extended to include lessons on constitutional history and law, while she also studied art and music. In addition she learned to ride and acquired her enthusiasm for horses. As she grew older she began to take part in public life, making her first broadcast at the age of 14. Early in 1945 she became a subaltern in the Auxiliary Territorial Service (ATS) and by the end of the war had reached the rank of Junior Commander.

The announcement of the engagement of Princess Elizabeth to Lieutenant Philip Mountbatten, the son of Prince Andrew of Greece and a great-great-grandson of Queen Victoria (now Prince Philip, Duke of Edinburgh) whom she had known for many years, was made in 1947. Their wedding took place in Westminster Abbey in November 1947. (Their Silver Wedding was celebrated in London in 1972.) She came to the throne on 6 February 1952 and was crowned on 2 June 1953. Since then, accompanied by the Duke of Edinburgh, she has undertaken innumerable tours throughout the Commonwealth at the invitation of the host governments, besides paying frequent visits to overseas countries outside the Commonwealth at the invitation of foreign heads of State. She has also made many visits throughout the United Kingdom, to fulfil engagements in connection with agriculture, industry, education, the arts, medicine and sport and as a means of keeping in touch with new developments in these fields. In 1977 her Silver Jubilee was celebrated in the United Kingdom and throughout the Commonwealth. Accompanied by the Duke of Edinburgh, the Queen travelled some 56,000 miles to share the anniversary with her people. Enormous crowds greeted them wherever they went, with millions more sharing in the celebrations through radio and television.

The Queen is an owner and breeder of thoroughbred horses, and often goes to race meetings to watch her horses run. She is also a frequent visitor at equestrian events.

The Duke of Edinburgh was born in 1921 and educated at Gordonstoun and the Royal Naval College, Dartmouth. He served at sea throughout the war, which he ended as a First Lieutenant. He ceased holding active naval appointments in 1951. The Duke has played an outstanding part in the nation's life and holds many important Service appointments and acts as patron or president of a large number of national organisations. In particular he interests himself in scientific and technological research and development, in the encouragement of sport, the welfare of young people and in the conservation and state of the environment. During the past 25 years the Duke has been closely involved in the development and growth of the Duke of Edinburgh's Award Scheme and devotes much time to meeting its participants and helpers. It is a programme of challenging leisure-time activities for young people from all over the Commonwealth, and encourages community service, adventure and personal achievement. Since 1965 well over 1·5 million young people have taken part. A keen sportsman, he formerly played polo regularly and has been President of the International Equestrian Federation since 1964.

The Queen's heir is Charles, Prince of Wales, who was born in 1948 and educated at Gordonstoun, at Geelong Grammar School in Australia, at Trinity College, Cambridge, and at Aberystwyth in the University of Wales. He has served in the

Royal Navy (besides obtaining his Wings at the Royal Air Force College at Cranwell) and since 1977 has been pursuing a programme of familiarisation with various aspects of public life in Britain, in particular industry and government, in addition to his normal round of royal duties. His engagement to Lady Diana Spencer was announced on 24 February 1981. The couple are to be married in St Paul's Cathedral, London, on 29 July 1981.

His younger brothers are Prince Andrew and Prince Edward, both educated at Gordonstoun. The former is at present serving with the Royal Navy. Their sister, Princess Anne, Mrs Mark Phillips, who is President of the Save the Children Fund and Chancellor of the University of London, is an expert horsewoman and a former Sportswoman of the Year. Her son Peter Phillips, the Queen's first grandchild, was born in 1977 and her daughter in 1981.

The Queen's mother, Queen Elizabeth the Queen Mother, the widow of the late King George VI, celebrated her eightieth birthday in 1980 amid scenes of great popular rejoicing. The Queen's only sister, Princess Margaret, Countess of Snowdon, has a son and a daughter by her former husband, the Earl of Snowdon. She is patron or president of a great number of public bodies, many of them concerned with youth activities, children's welfare, care of the sick and nursing organisations.

Among the Queen's other near relations are her first cousins—grandchildren of her grandfather King George V—the Dukes of Gloucester and Kent, Prince Michael and Princess Alexandra, the Hon Mrs Angus Ogilvy. All are married. The Duke of Gloucester is a professional architect and has married a Danish lady, the former Miss Birgitte van Deurs. Like the rest of the royal family, he carries out a substantial number of public duties and has many patronages. The Duke of Kent is a former serving Lieutenant-Colonel in the Army and is now Vice-Chairman of the British Overseas Trade Board. His wife is the former Miss Katharine Worsley. His brother, Prince Michael of Kent was until recently a Major in the Army. He is married to the former Baroness Marie-Christine von Reibnitz.

The Queen's Style and Titles

The development of the royal style and titles can be traced through a variety of changes reflecting historical events in the kingdoms of England and Scotland, in the union of those kingdoms in 1707, in the union with Ireland in 1801, and in the development of the Commonwealth. Today they are such as may be determined by the Crown under the authority of the Royal Titles Act 1953 and previous legislation. The Queen's title in the United Kingdom is: 'Elizabeth the Second, by the Grace of God of the United Kingdom of Great Britain and Northern Ireland and of Her other Realms and Territories Queen, Head of the Commonwealth, Defender of the Faith.' The form of the royal title is varied for the other member nations of the Commonwealth in which the Queen is head of State to suit the particular circumstances of each; all these forms include, however, the phrase 'Head of the Commonwealth'.

Succession

The title to the Crown derives partly from statute, partly from common law rules of descent. The English Act of Settlement 1700 laid down that lineal Protestant descendants of Princess Sophia[1] are alone eligible to succeed. This was affirmed by the Union of Scotland Act 1706. Subsequent Succession to the Crown Acts have confirmed this declaration; and, although the succession is not bound to continue

---

[1] *The Electress of Hanover, grand-daughter of James I.*

in its present line, it can only be altered (under a provision of the Statute of West-minster 1931) by common consent of all the member nations of the Commonwealth of which the Queen is Sovereign.

The sons of the Sovereign and their descendants have precedence over daughters in succeeding to the throne. However, the daughters take precedence over descend-ants of the Sovereign's brothers. When a daughter succeeds, she becomes Queen Regnant and the Crown's powers are vested in her as though she were king. While the consort of a king takes her husband's rank and style, the constitution has never given any special rank or privileges to the husband of a Queen.Regnant, and any honour granted to him comes from the Crown as 'the fountain of honour'. In practice he fills an important role in the life of the nation, as does the Duke of Edinburgh.[1]

Accession

The Sovereign succeeds to the throne as soon as his or her predecessor dies and there is no interregnum. (This automatic succession is summed up in the phrase, 'the King is dead; long live the King!') He or she is at once proclaimed at an Accession Council to which all members of the Privy Council[2] are summoned. Members of the House of Lords (including those bishops of the Church of England who sit in the House of Lords), the Lord Mayor and aldermen and other leading citizens of the City of London, and the High Commissioners in London of member nations of the Commonwealth are also invited to attend. The duration of Parliament is not affected by the death of a monarch.

Coronation

The Sovereign's coronation follows the accession, after an interval. It does not affect the legal powers of the Crown (King Edward VIII, for instance, was never crowned but reigned for nearly a year). It is a ceremony which has remained essentially the same over a thousand years, even if its details have often been modified to conform to the customs of the time. It consists broadly of recognition and acceptance of the new monarch by the people; the taking by the monarch of an oath of royal duties; the celebration of Holy Communion followed by anointing and crowning; and the rendering of homage by the Lords Spiritual and Temporal. The service used at the coronation of Queen Elizabeth II in 1953 was derived from that used at the coronation of King Edgar at Bath in 973.

The coronation service, conducted by the Archbishop of Canterbury, takes place at Westminster Abbey in the presence of representatives of the peers, the Commons and all the great public interests in the United Kingdom, the Prime Ministers and leading citizens of the Commonwealth countries, and representatives of other countries.

---

[1] *In 1952 it was announced that the Duke of Edinburgh should 'henceforth upon all occasions and in all meetings, except where otherwise provided by Act of Parliament, have, hold and enjoy place, pre-eminence and precedence next to Her Majesty'. In 1957 the Duke was given the title of a Prince of the United Kingdom.*

[2] *The Privy Council is formally the body on whose advice and through which the Sovereign exercises statutory and a number of prerogative powers (see p 8). It also has its own statutory duties, independent of the Sovereign's powers. Membership of the council is accorded by the Sovereign on the advice of the Prime Minister to people (including all British Cabinet Ministers) eminent in public affairs in many countries of the Commonwealth of which the Queen is Sovereign.*

The Royal Family's Styles and Titles

The first son (the Heir Apparent) born to a reigning monarch is by birth Duke of Cornwall in the peerage of England, and Duke of Rothesay, Earl of Carrick and Baron of Renfrew in the peerage of Scotland; he is also Lord of the Isles and Prince and Great Steward, or Seneschal, of Scotland. The titles 'Prince of Wales' and 'Earl of Chester' are created in each case, but have always been conferred on the Sovereign's eldest son; they were conferred on Prince Charles, the present heir, in 1958.

There is no style for an Heir or Heiress Presumptive (that is, the Prince or Princess who would succeed to the throne if the Sovereign had no son). It is usual for a Prince in that position to possess a royal dukedom. However, an Heiress Presumptive has no claim to the Duchy of Cornwall, nor can she become Princess of Wales.

The title of 'Royal Highness' is accorded by Letters Patent to all the monarch's children, the children of the monarch's sons, and the eldest living son of the eldest son of the Prince of Wales. The title is enjoyed by the wives of Royal Highnesses.

Under the Royal Marriages Act 1772 there are restrictions upon the right of descendants of King George II to marry without the monarch's consent. Until the age of 25 the consent is necessary (except in the case of the children of princesses who have married into foreign families), but after that age a marriage can take place without the consent after a year's notice to the Privy Council, unless Parliament expressly disapproves.

The House of Windsor

Until 1917, the royal family belonged to the House of Saxe-Coburg and Gotha. In the circumstances of the first world war (1914–18), however, it was considered appropriate for the King to adopt an English rather than a German name. He therefore adopted by proclamation the name of Windsor for Queen Victoria's descendants in the male line. In 1952 Queen Elizabeth II declared that she and her children should be known as the House and Family of Windsor, and that her descendants, other than female descendants who married and their descendants, should bear the name of Windsor. In 1960 the Queen declared that while she and her children would continue to be known as the House and Family of Windsor, her descendants, other than those entitled to the style and title of Royal Highness and Prince or Princess and females who married and their children, should bear the name of Mountbatten-Windsor.[1]

Regency and Counsellors of State

Provision has been made by statute for a regent to be appointed to perform the royal functions should the monarch be totally incapacitated, unavailable, or under 18 on succeeding to the throne. The declaration on the monarch's incapacity or unavailability has to be made by his or her consort, the Lord Chancellor, the Speaker of the House of Commons, the Lord Chief Justice and the Master of the Rolls (at least three must make the declaration). The regency continues until a declaration removing the impediment is made. A regent may exercise all the powers of a monarch except that he or she cannot assent to a Bill changing the order of succession to the throne or repealing the legislation securing the Scottish religion and church. At present the regent would be the Prince of Wales, then those in succession to the throne who are of age.

---

[1] *The surname of the Duke of Edinburgh is Mountbatten.*

In the case of the Queen's partial incapacity or absence abroad for more than a few days, she may appoint Counsellors of State by Letters Patent, and delegate to them certain functions in the United Kingdom, colonies, and certain other territories. (Commonwealth matters go direct to the Queen, wherever she may be.) Counsellors of State, of whom any two may deal with the routine signing of documents, cannot, for instance, dissolve Parliament (except on the Queen's express instructions) nor create peers. Under the present arrangements, Counsellors of State are appointed from among the Duke of Edinburgh, the Queen Mother, and the four adults next in succession.

The Queen's Representatives

In the Channel Islands, and in the Isle of Man, which are not part of the United Kingdom, but have a special relationship with it because of the antiquity of their connection with the Crown, the Queen is represented by a Lieutenant-Governor.

In the other Commonwealth countries of which she is Sovereign (see below), the Queen's representative is the Governor-General. He is appointed by her on the advice of the ministers of the country concerned and is completely independent of the British Government. In British dependencies the Queen is normally represented by Governors (in some cases by Commissioners, Administrators or Residents), who are responsible to the British Government for the good government of the countries concerned.

The Queen maintains direct contacts with the Governors-General and through the Foreign and Commonwealth Office with Governors, with British Ambassadors to foreign countries (who are accredited from the Queen to the head of State of the country concerned), and with the British High Commissioners in independent Commonwealth countries.

The Monarchy and the Commonwealth

Queen Elizabeth II is Queen not only of the United Kingdom and its dependencies but also of Australia, The Bahamas, Barbados, Canada, Fiji, Grenada, Jamaica, Mauritius, New Zealand, Papua New Guinea, Saint Lucia, St Vincent and the Grenadines, Solomon Islands, and Tuvalu. Of the other members of the Commonwealth, Bangladesh, Botswana, Cyprus, Dominica, The Gambia, Ghana, Guyana, India, Kenya, Kiribati, Malawi, Malta, Nauru, Nigeria, Seychelles, Sierra Leone, Singapore, Sri Lanka, Tanzania, Trinidad and Tobago, Uganda, Vanuatu, Zambia and Zimbabwe are republics, with a president as head of State; Lesotho, Malaysia, Swaziland and Tonga are monarchies; and Western Samoa has as its elected head of State a Paramount Chief.

Functions of the Monarch

The terms 'the Sovereign' (or 'Monarch') and 'the Crown', although related, are quite distinct. The Sovereign is the person on whom the Crown is constitutionally conferred, while the Crown (which represents both the Sovereign and the Government) is the symbol of supreme executive power. The Crown is vested in the Queen but in general its functions are exercised by ministers responsible to Parliament. The Queen reigns, but does not rule. The United Kingdom is governed by Her Majesty's Government in the name of the Queen. There are, however, many important acts of government which still require the participation of the Queen.

The Queen summons, prorogues (discontinues until the next session without dissolving) and dissolves Parliament. Normally she opens the new session with a speech from the throne outlining her Government's programme. When she is unable to be present, the Queen's speech is read by the Lord Chancellor. Before a Bill which has passed all its stages in both Houses of Parliament becomes a legal enactment, it must receive the Royal Assent, which is announced to both Houses. The Queen presides over meetings of the Privy Council at which, among other things, Orders in Council made under the royal prerogative (see below) or under statute are approved.

As the 'fountain of justice', the Queen can, on ministerial advice, pardon or show mercy to those convicted of crimes. All criminal prosecutions on indictment are brought in the name of the Crown. In law the Queen as a private person can do no wrong, nor, being immune from civil or criminal proceedings, can she be sued in courts of law. This personal immunity, which does not extend to other members of the royal family, was expressly retained in the Crown Proceedings Act 1947, which for the first time allowed the Crown (in effect, a government department or minister) to be sued directly in civil proceedings.

As the 'fountain of honour', the Queen confers peerages, knighthoods and other honours[1] (on the recommendation of the Prime Minister who usually seeks the view of others). She makes appointments to many important state offices, although on the advice of the Prime Minister or, in some cases, the appropriate Cabinet Minister. She appoints and dismisses, for instance, government ministers, judges (the dismissal of judges is regulated by statute), members of the diplomatic corps and colonial officials. As Commander-in-Chief of the armed services she appoints officers, and as Supreme Governor of the established Church of England she makes appointments to its bishoprics and some other senior offices.

In international affairs, the Queen (to whom foreign diplomatic representatives in London present their credentials) has the power to conclude treaties, to declare war and to make peace, to recognise foreign states and governments, and to annexe and cede territory.

The Royal Prerogative

These and similar functions involve exercising the royal prerogative—broadly speaking, the collection of residual powers left in the hands of the Crown. Present-day prerogative rights and duties of the Crown, in many cases ill-defined, are

---

[1] *Most honours are conferred by the Sovereign on the advice of the Prime Minister. A few are conferred by the Sovereign personally: the Most Noble Order of the Garter, the Most Noble and Most Ancient Order of the Thistle, the Order of Merit and the Royal Victorian Order. Normally, honours lists are published twice a year—at the New Year and to mark the Queen's official birthday in June. For further information see COI reference paper Honours and Titles in Britain, R5456/76.*

remnants of immunities and powers possessed by medieval kings, both as chief feudal lords and as heads of the State. Nowadays the prerogative mainly comprises executive government powers the exercise of which is controlled by constitutional conventions.[1]

With rare exceptions (as in the appointment of the Prime Minister), acts involving the royal prerogative are nowadays performed by ministers who are responsible to Parliament and can be questioned about a particular policy. It is not necessary to have Parliament's authority to exercise these powers, although Parliament has the power to restrict or abolish a prerogative right. The Crown is not bound by an Act of Parliament in the absence of any express words to the contrary.

The most common ways in which the royal will can be constitutionally expressed are: by Order in Council made 'by and with the advice of the Privy Council'; by Order, Commission or Warrant signed personally by the Queen and generally bearing the signature of one or more responsible Secretary of State; or by Proclamation, Writs, Letters Patent, or other documents under the Great Seal affixed by the Lord Chancellor[2] in obedience to a Royal Warrant countersigned by a Secretary of State.

Relations with the Prime Minister and Government

An important function of the Sovereign is appointing the Prime Minister. By convention the Sovereign invites the leader of the party which commands a majority in the House of Commons to form a government. If no party has a majority, or if the party having a majority has no recognised leader, the Queen has the duty of selecting a Prime Minister. In such circumstances she would be entitled to consult anyone she wished.

Ministerial responsibility for the exercise of powers by the Crown does not detract from the importance of the participation of the Sovereign in the smooth working of government, for the Queen must be informed and consulted on every aspect of the national life to the widest possible extent, and is free to put forward her own views in private for the consideration of her ministers. The Sovereign has, in the words of Walter Bagehot writing in 1867, 'the right to be consulted, the right to encourage' and 'the right to warn'.

The Queen's closest official contacts are with the Prime Minister (who has an audience of the Queen on average once a week when the Queen is in London), and, through him or her, with the Cabinet. She sees other ministers as well, generally to discuss the affairs of their departments, and sees all Cabinet papers, the Cabinet agenda in advance, and the minutes of the meetings of the Cabinet and of its committees. She may discuss memoranda with the ministers responsible and, if necessary, seek further information on any topic from departments through her Private Secretary (see p 18). The Queen receives copies of all important Foreign and Commonwealth Office telegrams and dispatches. She also receives a daily summary of parliamentary proceedings prepared for her by a member of the Government (the Vice-Chamberlain of the Household—see p 17).

The Queen is ultimately responsible for dissolving Parliament, normally done at the request of the Prime Minister.

---

[1] *Rules and practices which are not part of the law in the sense that violation of them would lead to proceedings in a court of law, but which are regarded none the less as indispensable to the machinery of government.*

[2] *Or, on Scottish documents, the Great Seal of Scotland affixed by the Keeper of the Great Seal (the Secretary of State for Scotland).*

The Queen's Public Functions

As the inheritor of a monarchical tradition which has endured for over a thousand years, the Queen is not just the head of State, but the living symbol of national unity. She provides the natural focus for popular loyalty. Ceremonial has always been associated with British kings and queens and, in spite of the changed outlook of both the Sovereign and the people, many traditional ceremonies and customs are retained. Royal marriages and funerals are still marked by impressive ceremonial; and the birthday of the Sovereign is officially celebrated every June by Trooping the Colour on Horse Guards Parade. Royal processions add significance to such occasions as the opening of Parliament, when the Queen drives in state from Buckingham Palace to Westminster, and the arrival of visiting heads of State.

Royal ceremonial arouses wide popular interest and is a vital factor in the relations between Sovereign and people. The relationship is fostered by many means, including modern mass communications media, which have played an important part in bringing the Queen closer to her subjects. Films like *The Royal Family* and *Royal Heritage* and the coverage of such events as the Silver Jubilee celebrations of 1977 have been seen by many millions of television viewers throughout the world. (It has been estimated that 500 million people will watch the marriage of Prince Charles to Lady Diana Spencer.) Hundreds of royal visits to various parts of the country for public functions keep the royal family in close touch with new developments. These often involve visits lasting more than one day, and sometimes centre on an international or national event such as the Royal Agricultural Show or more usually an event of local importance like the opening of a new bridge or hospital. There are also royal film, variety and concert performances in aid of charity, and visits to schools, universities, hospitals and factories. The Queen visits many important sporting events, and, as an owner and breeder of thoroughbred racehorses, frequently watches her horses run at race meetings. She attends the 'Derby' at Epsom (one of the classic 'flat' horse-races) and the summer race meeting at Ascot.

In addition to being head of all three armed services, the Queen is Colonel-in-Chief of several regiments and corps in Britain and in other Commonwealth countries. (As Princess Elizabeth, she served in the Auxiliary Territorial Service.) Apart from regular visits to units of the armed forces, she is able to keep in touch with the work and interests of the Royal Navy and the Royal Air Force through the royal yacht and the Queen's Flight (see p 25).

The Queen holds about 14 investitures a year at which she bestows the awards conferred on both civilians and members of the armed forces. She presents annually some 3,000 orders, decorations and medals. Investitures are also conducted by the Queen on her visits to other Commonwealth countries. Some 30,000 people from all sections of the community (including visitors from overseas) attend royal garden parties each year. Three are held at Buckingham Palace, one at Holyroodhouse, Edinburgh, and there is often a special party in each place for an organisation such as the Royal British Legion or the National Federation of Women's Institutes. Regular luncheon parties held by the Queen are attended by people distinguished in widely different spheres. Other regular public occasions include services of the Order of the Garter, the Order of the Thistle and other Orders, the Remembrance Day ceremony at the Cenotaph in Whitehall and various services at St Paul's Cathedral and Westminster Abbey. The Queen presents the Maundy money at Westminster Abbey or in one of the other cathedrals or abbeys in the country.

One of the most important duties performed by the Sovereign is to act as host to the heads of State of Commonwealth and other countries when they visit the United Kingdom. When a State visit is involved, guests stay at Buckingham Palace,

Windsor Castle or the Palace of Holyroodhouse. Their entertainment includes banquets, receptions, often a special ballet or opera performance and visits to places of particular interest throughout the country. On the many other occasions when heads of State visit the United Kingdom, either privately or for official purposes, they are nearly always entertained or received by the Queen. Luncheons are frequently held for other distinguished visitors from overseas.

The overseas tours which the Queen and the Duke of Edinburgh make together —nowadays one of their most important functions—fall into two broad categories. There are visits to other Commonwealth countries, made at the invitation of the host government; and there are State visits to countries outside the Commonwealth at the invitation of a foreign head of State and accepted on the advice of the British Government. No previous Sovereign has undertaken overseas visits on such a scale. The Duke of Edinburgh has also visited many countries overseas by himself, both as the Queen's representative and in his own right.

It is customary at Christmas for the Queen to speak on radio and television to all the people of the Commonwealth as their head.

Other Members of the Royal Family

The contribution by other members of the royal family in supplementing the Queen's public functions is of the greatest importance. They too have a heavy schedule of official appearances, both national and international. They help to entertain visiting heads of State and pay official visits overseas, occasionally representing the Queen, though usually in their own right in connection with an organisation or a cause with which they are associated. They serve as patrons or presidents of many of the most prominent institutions and charities in Britain and are constantly making public appearances. It has recently been estimated, for example, that in 1980 (the year in which she celebrated her eightieth birthday) Queen Elizabeth the Queen Mother carried out 66 official visits, opening ceremonies and other appearances, including charity galas and premieres. She also attended 33 receptions, lunches, dinners and banquets, and gave 16 audiences.

Royal Income and Expenditure

More than three-quarters of the expenditure arising from the official duties of the royal family is met by public departments—including, for example, the costs of the royal yacht *Britannia*, the Queen's Flight, travel by train, the upkeep of the royal palaces, and State visits overseas.

The remainder of the Queen's expenditure is financed from three sources. First, the Queen's Civil List (see below), a payment from public funds approved by Parliament, finances the costs of running the Royal Household and other expenses incurred in the course of her official duties as head of State. Secondly, the Privy Purse, financed from the revenues of the Duchy of Lancaster,[1] meets the cost of: private expenditure arising from the Queen's responsibilities as head of State (for example, the purchase of clothes, robes, uniforms, etc); creating a pension fund for past and present employees not otherwise provided for; the maintenance of the Queen's private residences at Sandringham in Norfolk and Balmoral in Scotland; charitable subscriptions and donations; and staff welfare and amenities. The Privy Purse has also met substantial Civil List deficits in the past, and contributes to the official expenses of other members of the royal family. Finally, the Queen's personal expenditure as a private individual is met from her own personal resources.

The royal palaces, together with the Crown jewels and the royal collections of art, stamps and books, are vested in the Queen as Sovereign but cannot be disposed of—they must be passed on to her successor. They are therefore not her personal property. There are also other items—for example, of jewellery—which the Queen regards as heirlooms and not at her free personal disposal.

The Civil List

The basic Civil List is paid automatically by the Treasury from the Consolidated Fund under an Act of Parliament, normally passed within six months of the beginning of a reign, which continues in force for six months after the death of the Sovereign (although a revision may take place in the course of a reign). In exchange, the Sovereign surrenders to the Exchequer the revenue from the Crown Estate[2] and certain hereditary revenues.

The Civil List covers expenditure on the salaries and expenses of the Royal Household (staff of the Household are almost entirely paid and pensioned[3] on a basis analogous to that in the Civil Service), and royal bounty, alms and special services. About three-quarters of the Civil List provision is required for the salaries of those who deal with, among other things, State papers and correspondence, organising State occasions, visits and other public engagements in Britain and overseas,

---

[1] *The Duchy of Lancaster comprises some 52,000 acres (21,000 hectares), mostly of farmland and moorland.*

[2] *The Crown Estate, comprising properties throughout Great Britain, traditionally belongs to the Sovereign 'in right of the Crown', and is quite separate from his or her personal property. Under the Crown Estate Act 1961 management of the estate is the responsibility of commissioners appointed by the Sovereign on the advice of the Prime Minister. An annual report on the estate is submitted to Parliament.*

[3] *Payment of pensions to retired staff of the Royal Household is made by the Treasury direct from the Consolidated Fund. Parliament has also authorised payment of 'Civil List pensions' which are nowadays awarded at the discretion of the Prime Minister for services to science, literature, music or the arts.*

Three generations of the Royal Family: from left to right, the Duke of Edinburgh, Prince Edward, the Prince of Wales, the Queen, Prince Andrew, and Princess Anne with her son Peter Phillips (the Queen's first grandchild).

The picture was taken in the grounds of Balmoral Castle, the Queen's private residence in Scotland.

Facing page. Buckingham Palace, the Queen's London home.

Previous page. The Queen and the Duke of Edinburgh in the Long Gallery of Windsor Castle.

In the Music Room at Buckingham Palace during the State Visit of the President of Nigeria. In the foreground are Queen Elizabeth the Queen Mother, President Shehu Shagari, the Queen and the Duke of Edinburgh. Behind are the Prince of Wales, Princess Michael of Kent and the Prince's fiancée, Lady Diana Spencer.

The Queen and the Duke of Edinburgh with Pope John Paul II during a visit to the Vatican.

Facing page. The Queen's Speech at the State Opening of Parliament outlines the Government's programme for the coming session.

Press Association

Anwar Hussein

The Queen visits the
Yorkshire coalfield and
the Prince of Wales a
North Sea oil rig. Britain is
now self-sufficient in
energy in net terms and
richer in energy resources
than other European
Community countries.

The Queen being shown airborne radar equipments when opening Ferranti's new complex at Edinburgh.

The Duke of Edinburgh inspects the flight deck layout of the BAe 146 short-haul airliner being developed by British Aerospace.

Victoria 1837–1901

Edward VII 1901–1910

George V 1910–1936

Edward VIII 1936

George VI 1936–1952

Elizabeth II 1952–

Facing page. British monarchs from Victoria to Elizabeth II.

The Royal Arms (see p 23).

The Crown Jewels, displayed in the Tower of London, all have ritual significance in the Coronation ceremony. The crown is that of St. Edward, which is used for the crowning of the Sovereign. Also shown are the Jewelled State Sword, the two sceptres, the gold Ampulla in the shape of an eagle, the Anointing Spoon, the Coronation Ring and the Golden Bracelets.

HONI SOIT QUI MAL Y PENSE

DIEU ET MON DROIT

The Prince of Wales at a youth centre at Derby in central England.

Facing page. The royal 'walkabout' has become a familiar feature of Britain's monarchy, as on this occasion during celebrations to mark the Queen's Silver Jubilee.

The Prince of Wales examining BL's Mini Metro, which was launched in Britain at the end of 1980 and went on sale in Western Europe in April 1981.

Every year some 30,000 people from all sections of the community, including visitors from overseas, attend royal garden parties such as this one at Buckingham Palace.

Facing page. The Queen with members of the Privy Council at Buckingham Palace after giving her formal consent to the marriage of the Prince of Wales and Lady Diana Spencer. Among those present for this first photograph of the Privy Council to be taken in the United Kingdom are the Prince of Wales, the Prime Minister and other leading political figures, the Archbishop of Canterbury and Commonwealth Privy Counsellors.

Facing page. A family group at Buckingham Palace on the Queen Mother's eightieth birthday in 1980. On the left are her daughters, Princess Margaret and the Queen, on the right her grand-daughter Princess Anne. Behind, standing from the left, are Viscount Linley and Lady Sarah Armstrong-Jones (Princess Margaret's children), Prince Andrew, the Duke of Edinburgh, the Prince of Wales, Prince Edward and Captain Mark Phillips (Princess Anne's husband).

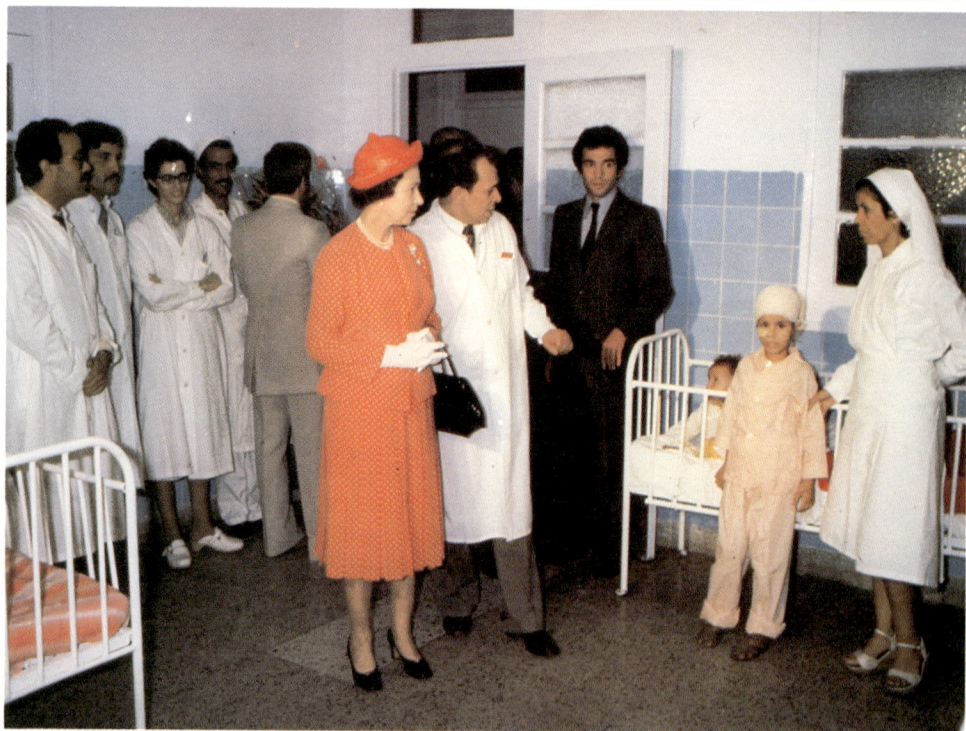

Princess Anne, President of the Save the Children Fund, visits Swindon in connection with children's charities.

Prince Andrew, the Queen's second son, has obtained his wings as a helicopter pilot.

Facing page. The Duchess of Kent in New Zealand.

Facing page. The Queen visits the Mustapha Hospital in Algeria to meet earthquake victims.

Overleaf. When the heir to the throne, Prince Charles, and Lady Diana Spencer are married in St Paul's Cathedral in July 1981 it will be the first wedding of a Prince of Wales for over a century.

and arranging the interviews and investitures undertaken by the Queen, and those who clean and staff the Royal buildings and who work in the Royal Mews.

Because of the rising costs of running the Royal Household in times of inflation, and despite every effort to make economies, it became impractical to settle the amount of the Civil List by legislation at relatively infrequent intervals. Accordingly, the Civil List Act 1975 established a system whereby payments additional to those provided under the Civil List Act 1972 could be made, subject to annual authorisation by Parliament, together with other departmental expenditure.

Under this Act, the Treasury makes annual payments from money provided by Parliament to supplement the Queen's Civil List, annuities to certain named members of the royal family (see below), contributions towards the expenses of other members of the royal family, and Civil List pensions. The payments are by way of grant-in-aid to the Royal Trustees (the Prime Minister, the Chancellor of the Exchequer and the Keeper of the Privy Purse) and are subject to the normal parliamentary 'supply' procedure for the approval of government expenditure. The Royal Trustees generally review the working of the Civil List system at least once every ten years, and report to Parliament.

This change in the machinery for determining Civil List payments was accompanied by an offer from the Queen, which the Government accepted, to pay from 1976 onwards an annual contribution equivalent to the provision made from public funds towards the official expenses of members of the royal family for whom Parliament had made no specific provision (at present the Duke of Gloucester, the Duke of Kent and Princess Alexandra).

Provision for Members of the Royal Family

The amounts payable from central funds under the Civil List Acts to members of the royal family are as follows in the calendar year 1981:

The Queen's Civil List	£3,260,200
Queen Elizabeth the Queen Mother	£286,000
The Duke of Edinburgh	£160,000
Princess Anne	£100,000
Princess Margaret	£98,000
Princess Alice, Duchess of Gloucester	£40,000
The Duke of Gloucester	£78,000
The Duke of Kent	£106,000
Princess Alexandra	£101,000

The 1972 Act also provides that the younger sons of the Queen (Prince Andrew and Prince Edward) should receive £20,000 annually on reaching the age of 18, and before marriage. This would be increased to £50,000 after marriage. Prince Andrew was 18 in February 1978, but only received £10,500 of his allocation for 1981, the balance being accumulated by the Royal Trustees.

In addition the Act provides that a widow of the Prince of Wales would be entitled to an allowance of £60,000 a year and that the annual amount payable to a future wife of a younger son of the Queen in the event of her surviving her husband would be £20,000.

Any of these payments may be supplemented by the Royal Trustees under the provisions of the 1975 Act. The greater part is paid to meet official expenses incurred in carrying out public duties.

Parliament makes no special provision for the Prince of Wales, who is entitled, as Duke of Cornwall, to the net revenues of the estate of the Duchy of Cornwall—

about 129,000 acres (52,205 hectares) in south-west England and London. At the age of 21 he became entitled to these revenues but voluntarily undertook to surrender half to the Exchequer. This arrangement is subject to review on his marriage or some other change of circumstances.

Taxation

As part of the royal prerogative the Queen does not pay tax—either on her private wealth and income, or on the Queen's Civil List—unless Parliament decides otherwise. This immunity extends to income from the Duchy of Lancaster.

The income and property of the Duchy of Cornwall are similarly exempt from income tax, capital gains tax and capital transfer tax. Any other income or property of the Prince of Wales is taxed in the ordinary way as though it were his total income or property.

The Civil List annuities payable to members of the royal family are exempt from income tax either wholly or in part, only to the extent that they are used to meet official expenses incurred in carrying out public duties.

Payments by the Royal Trustees to cover the official expenses of other members of the royal family, in accordance with normal taxation practice, do not rank as income for tax purposes.

Departmental Votes

More than three-quarters of all expenditure arising from the official duties of the royal family is borne on departmental votes. The costs of the royal yacht *Britannia* and of the Queen's Flight of aircraft (see p 25) are met by the Ministry of Defence. Travel by train on official business by the royal family and staff of the Royal Household is paid for by the Department of the Environment. Other items of expenditure met by government departments include the cost of official travel overseas and the provision of service equerries. Postal services are provided free of charge by the Post Office; the cost of telecommunications is met by the Department of the Environment.

The Royal Palaces

The Department of the Environment is also responsible for the upkeep of the royal palaces: Buckingham Palace, Windsor Castle, St James's Palace, Hampton Court Palace, Kensington Palace, Kew Palace and the Palace of Holyroodhouse in Edinburgh. Of these, Buckingham Palace, Windsor Castle and the Palace of Holyroodhouse are State residences of the Sovereign. At the Queen's private residences, Balmoral and Sandringham, however, the only costs met by the Department are those for the fuel and electricity required when the court is in residence.

Buckingham Palace, built on the site of a house owned by the Duke of Buckingham, has been the Sovereign's London residence since 1837. The present building was erected in the eighteenth century and re-designed in 1825; it was refronted in Portland stone in 1913.

Windsor Castle has been a principal residence of the Sovereign for nearly 900 years. Built by William the Conqueror (1066–87) and extended in the fourteenth and fifteenth centuries, it was extensively restored by George IV (1820–30). Notable features are St George's Chapel (fifteenth and sixteenth centuries) and the State Apartments, containing many historic and artistic treasures.

The Sovereign's State residence in Scotland is the Palace of Holyroodhouse on the site of an abbey founded in 1128. The original early sixteenth-century royal palace was largely destroyed by Cromwell's soldiers in 1650 and the present building dates from the seventeenth century.

The importance in former times of St James's Palace in London is reflected in the fact that ambassadors of foreign states are still accredited to the Court of St James's.

Balmoral Castle was built by Queen Victoria and Prince Albert and first used as a royal residence in 1855. The Sandringham estate was bought by Edward VII (then Prince of Wales) in 1863, and in 1871 the existing house was pulled down and replaced by one in red brick. Substantial alterations, considerably reducing the size of the house, have been undertaken.

The Royal Household

Great Officers of State

The royal household was originally the centre of the system of government. The leading dignitaries of the palace—the Sovereign's closest advisers—were, by the nature of the executive power directly exercised by the monarch, also the principal administrators of the State. With the development of ministerial responsibility for executive acts, many leading members of the original royal household of England—the Lord Chancellor, the Lord President of the Council, the Lord Privy Seal and the Secretary of State (an office now divided between a number of ministers)—became members of the political administration and entirely divorced from household duties. The ancient office of Lord High Treasurer has been put in commission,[1] while two other offices—those of the Lord High Steward and Lord High Constable—are now granted only for the single day of a coronation. While no Great Officer of State retains household functions, two (the Lord Great Chamberlain and the Earl Marshal) retain duties in connection with royal ceremonial.

The Lord Great Chamberlain

The office of Lord Great Chamberlain dates back to the reign of King Henry I (1100–35). At present, the Cholmondeley family holds the office every alternate reign, and the Ancaster and Carrington families each hold it every fourth reign.

The Lord Great Chamberlain was originally head of the Sovereign's personal household and all royal palaces. Few of these duties are nowadays attached to the office, but the holder is responsible for the arrangements when the Sovereign attends Parliament (see p 8), and at the coronation ceremony, when he stands on the left of the Sovereign in Westminster Abbey, fastens the clasp of the Imperial Mantle after investiture, and arrays the Sovereign in purple robes before the procession out of the Abbey.

Since each Lord Great Chamberlain enters upon his duties immediately a new reign begins, he has to arrange, in conjunction with the Department of the Environment, for the Lying-in-State of the dead monarch at Westminster Hall.

The Earl Marshal

The office of Earl Marshal of England also originated in the reign of King Henry I. It has been hereditary in the family of the Duke of Norfolk since 1672.

The Earl Marshal is head of the College of Arms and is also responsible for the arrangement of coronations, royal funerals and other State functions.

Officers of the Royal Household

Certain offices have become obsolete with the passage of time, and a few have been created comparatively recently to meet modern requirements. A number, however, have been retained since Plantagenet and Tudor times, although the duties attached to them are now very different.

Although the ministerial holders of Great Offices of State are no longer members of the household, certain officers have governmental, as well as household, duties to perform. The Treasurer, Comptroller and Vice-Chamberlain of the Household all

---

[1] *That is to say, functions are carried out by a body of deputies (the Lords Commissioners of the Treasury).*

act as Government Whips in the House of Commons, and the Captain of the Gentlemen-at-Arms, the Captain of the Yeomen of the Guard and three of the five non-permanent Lords-in-Waiting act as Government Whips in the House of Lords. Although the Lord Chamberlain, Lord Steward, Master of the Horse and the non-political Lords-in-Waiting have, since 1924, been appointed by the personal choice of the Sovereign, they are appointed on condition that they do not vote against the Government of the day in the House of Lords (of which they are all members).

Broadly speaking, the royal household consists of a number of departments and offices, each under a principal household officer.

The Lord Steward

For centuries the Lord Steward was responsible for the Palace below-stairs, and managed the catering arrangements for State banquets, Courts and all other forms of royal entertaining, together with appointing and superintending numerous people in the service of the Sovereign, and the payment of all household expenses. Nowadays, these functions are carried out by the department of the Master of the Household, who is a permanent officer. The Lord Steward, appointed by the Sovereign, still retains the titular authority and, on ceremonial occasions, bears a white staff as an emblem of his position. The Coroner of the Household, who exercises jurisdiction in the royal palaces and in any other place where the Sovereign may be staying, is appointed by the Lord Steward.

The Treasurer and the Comptroller

The offices of Treasurer of the Household and Comptroller of the Household are now political appointments and change with a change of government.

The Lord Chamberlain

The Lord Chamberlain was originally a deputy of the Lord Great Chamberlain, but later became independent and took over all ceremonial duties relating to the household as such. He is the senior officer of the household, and carries a white staff and wears a golden key on ceremonial occasions as a symbol of his office.

The Lord Chamberlain is in charge of Court ceremonial, including arrangements for royal weddings, for royal garden parties, for ceremonial connected with State visits to the United Kingdom and for communication with Commonwealth countries about ceremonial matters. He acts as the Queen's emissary to the House of Lords.

The other functions of the Lord Chamberlain include: carrying out the wishes of the Sovereign in the appointment of royal chaplains, royal physicians and surgeons, and other household officers; superintending the royal collection of works of art; and supervising the internal administration of certain of the royal residences.

The Vice-Chamberlain's appointment is now a political one and he takes no part in the work of the Lord Chamberlain's office. During parliamentary sessions the Vice-Chamberlain sends the Queen a daily confidential report on parliamentary proceedings.

The Lord Chamberlain's office consists of: the Comptroller and his staff, who assist the Lord Chamberlain with the supervision of the household and ceremonies; the Gentleman Usher of the Black Rod, who is the Principal Usher in the kingdom, and has the duty of summoning the Commons and their Speaker to the House of Lords (where he is responsible for maintaining order) when they are required to hear a speech from the throne, for example; other Gentlemen Ushers in attendance upon the Sovereign; the Constable and Deputy Constable of Windsor Castle; the

Ecclesiastical Household (see below); the Marshal of the Diplomatic Corps, who is responsible for ceremonial in receiving foreign ambassadors; Lords-in-Waiting; the Serjeants-at-Arms; the Pages of Honour, who are boys who wait upon the Sovereign on State occasions; the Keeper of the Jewel House, Tower of London; the Master of the Queen's Music; the Poet Laureate; the Art Surveyors; the Bargemaster; and the Keeper of the Queen's Swans.

The Ecclesiastical Household consists of the Clerk of the Closet, usually a bishop, whose traditional duty it was 'to attend at the right hand of the Sovereign in the Royal Closet during Divine Service to resolve such doubts as may arise concerning spiritual matters'; the Deputy Clerk to the Closet; the Dean and Sub-Dean of the Chapels Royal[1] and domestic chaplains and chaplains-in-ordinary. The chaplains-in-ordinary are not concerned solely with the Court; they have a rota of attendance to conduct divine service and preach at royal chapels.

The Master of the Horse

The Master of the Horse is the third dignitary at Court. Formerly the holder of a powerful office, he is now in charge of the Sovereign's stables, and responsible for providing the horses, carriages and motor cars required for processions and for the daily needs of the royal family. His day-to-day duties are carried out by his deputy— the Chief or Crown Equerry. The Master of the Horse rides immediately behind the Sovereign in State processions.

Most equerries of the household—regular, extra or honorary—are officers of the armed services. There are usually two regular equerries, one of whom is always in waiting upon the Sovereign.

The Private Secretary

Each Sovereign appoints his or her own Private Secretary. The Private Secretary, helped by a Deputy and an Assistant Private Secretary, deals with all the correspondence between the Queen and her ministers, whether of the British or other Commonwealth Governments. Government appointments for which the Queen's approval is required go to the Queen through her Private Secretary. The Private Secretary is also concerned with the Queen's speeches, messages and private papers, and is responsible for her engagements, both in the United Kingdom and overseas, for the office of the Press Secretary and for the royal archives.

The Keeper of the Privy Purse and Treasurer to the Sovereign

The Keeper of the Privy Purse and Treasurer to the Sovereign deals with payments made from the Sovereign's private resources as well as official expenditure and the payment of salaries and wages to the Sovereign's officers and servants. His department consists of the Privy Purse Office, the Treasurer's Office and the Royal Almonry, at the head of which is the High Almoner—an ecclesiastical appointment usually held by a bishop—who in former times was responsible for the almsgiving of the Sovereign.

---

[1] *A chapel royal is a chapel attached to the Court (historically it moved from place to place with the Court), and is subject, not to the jurisdiction of a bishop, but (in England) to that of the Dean of the Chapels Royal. There are chapels royal at St James's Palace, Hampton Court Palace and the Tower of London. In Scotland there is a chapel royal at the Palace of Holyroodhouse. Many other chapels and churches have special associations with the royal family.*

Ladies-in-Waiting

The Mistress of the Robes is the senior lady of the Queen's Household, and usually a Duchess. She is responsible for arranging the rota for the Ladies-in-Waiting and is in attendance on the Queen on State occasions, sometimes accompanying her on other important visits. At one time the Mistress of the Robes was an important person in national politics, but nowadays the appointment has no political significance, and the Queen names who she pleases.

There are two Ladies of the Bedchamber who attend the Queen on important public occasions, but do not go into waiting regularly. There are four Women of the Bedchamber, who, in turn for a fortnight at a time, attend the Queen on all public and semi-private engagements, make her personal arrangements, do shopping and make inquiries about people who are ill. They also deal with some of the Queen's correspondence—mainly answering all the letters written to her by children. There are three extra Women of the Bedchamber who are in waiting occasionally.

Other Appointments

Others associated with the Royal Household are the Sovereign's Aides-de-Camp, who are appointed from the naval, military and air forces, and Her Majesty's Representative at Ascot, who has a duty in respect of Royal Ascot,[1] including the supervision of the issue of tickets for the Royal Enclosure.

Kings, Heralds and Pursuivants of Arms[2]

The College of Arms in England and Wales is a corporation of 13 members— three Kings of Arms; six Heralds; and four Pursuivants. All are members of the royal household, appointed by the Queen, on the nomination of the Earl Marshal. The history of the heralds as members of the household goes back to the thirteenth century, but they were not constituted into a corporation until 1484, and the present corporation dates from 1555.

The Kings of Arms are Garter, Clarenceux, and Norroy and Ulster.[3] Garter was created in 1415 by King Henry V. He is both King of Arms of the Most Noble Order of the Garter and Principal King of Arms. He is responsible to the Earl Marshal for the conduct of the ceremonial introduction of a peer in the House of Lords. Clarenceux and Norroy were constituted by the time of King Edward III (1327–77), the province of the former comprising all land to the south, and of the latter all land to the north, of the River Trent. The Kings of Arms grant arms by Letters Patent.

The six Heralds are Windsor, Chester, Lancaster, York, Richmond and Somerset, who take precedence according to seniority in office. The four Pursuivants are Rouge Croix, Bluemantle, Rouge Dragon and Portcullis.

In addition to verifying and recording arms and genealogies, the Kings of Arms, Heralds and Pursuivants attend upon the Sovereign on ceremonial occasions such as coronations, State funerals, State openings of Parliament and ceremonies connected with the Order of the Garter.

In Scotland, similar functions are performed by Lord Lyon King of Arms, who has under him three Heralds—Marchmont, Rothesay and Albany—and four

---

[1] Founded in 1711 by Queen Anne who initiated the traditional State drive to the course which now takes place on each day of the race meeting in June.

[2] For information about the royal arms, see p 23.

[3] The office of Ulster King of Arms was transferred from Dublin to London (being united with that of Norroy in 1943).

Pursuivants—Kintyre, Carrick, Unicorn and Falkland (Pursuivant Extraordinary). The Officers of Arms of Scotland are not under the jurisdiction of the Earl Marshal. Since 1867 they have been appointed by the Government.

Royal Bodyguards and Household Troops

The practice of maintaining bodyguards round the Sovereign is said to have been introduced into England by King Canute (1016–35). Royal bodyguards are now divided into two groups. The first includes the non-combatant personal bodyguards: the Honourable Corps of Gentlemen-at-Arms; the Yeomen of the Guard; and, in Scotland, the Royal Company of Archers. The second includes those regiments of the Regular Army which have the special duty of guarding the Sovereign and the metropolis of London: the Household Cavalry and the Foot Guards.

The Gentlemen-at-Arms

The Honourable Corps of Gentlemen-at-Arms is termed the 'nearest guard' since it is the guard in the closest personal attendance upon the Sovereigns of England. It was created in 1509, but did not acquire its present designation until the reign of King William IV (1830–37). In its early days the guard fought in a number of battles and distinguished itself, notably at the Battle of Spurs (1513). Its principal function, however, was to attend the Sovereign on all occasions of State ceremonial, and it has continued to do so ever since. Today, the Corps is under the administrative control of the Lord Chamberlain; it attends the Sovereign on all State occasions, and is present at many palace functions.

The Honourable Corps of Gentlemen-at-Arms now numbers 28 Gentlemen (one, the Harbinger, in the old days sent in advance to secure lodging), and four officers. The Gentlemen have all been distinguished officers of the Army or Royal Marines. The officers of the corps consist of a Clerk of the Cheque and Adjutant, a Standard Bearer, a Lieutenant and a Captain, the last of whom must be a peer and a member of the Government in power.

All appointments to the Honourable Corps are made by the Sovereign, from whom officers receive their sticks, the Captain's appointment being on ministerial advice, the rest by the Sovereign's prerogative. The headquarters and orderly room are in Engine Court, St James's Palace, London.

The Yeomen of the Guard

The Yeomen of the Guard form a permanent military corps which has been in attendance on the Sovereign for more than 450 years. Some remnants of an even older corps exist in the persons of the Serjeants-at-Arms—royal household officials on duty in the Houses of Parliament, and on ceremonial occasions in attendance on the Sovereign.

The original duties of the corps were very wide. As the Sovereign's personal servants its members were responsible for attending upon the Sovereign day and night, at home and abroad; and for his safety on journeys, on the battlefield and within the palace walls. At one time their duties extended to making and examining the Sovereign's bed, and these duties are perpetuated in the ranks of Yeoman Bed Goer and Yeoman Bed Hanger. They also cooked the Sovereign's food and carried the dishes to his table—a service now symbolised by the Exon-in-Waiting standing behind the Sovereign's chair at State banquets.

Most of the guard's present duties are purely ceremonial. They include attendance on guard at the reception of foreign dignitaries and heads of State; at State banquets;

at State balls and gala operas; at the ceremony of the distribution of Maundy money on Maundy Thursday (a ceremony first attended by the Yeomen of the Guard in 1486); at the Epiphany offerings of gold, frankincense and myrrh in the Chapel Royal, St James's Palace; at Westminster Hall during a royal Lying-in-State; and at the searching of the vaults of the Houses of Parliament at the opening of each session—a duty dating from the Gunpowder Plot of 1605.

All officers of the Yeomen of the Guard (except the Captain) and all non-commissioned officers and yeomen must have served in the Regular Army, Royal Marines or Royal Air Force. They are selected for distinguished conduct and their pay is looked upon as a pension. Officers must have held the rank of captain or over, and yeomen that of sergeant or warrant officer. The corps has a permanent orderly room in St James's Palace, London, where the routine is carried on by the Clerk of the Cheque and Adjutant.

The Yeomen Warders of the Tower of London are not Yeomen of the Guard. They derive from the 12 yeomen King Henry VIII left behind in the Tower on giving it up as a permanent residence. When the Tower finally ceased to be a royal palace, these yeomen became warders. Nowadays, they are a distinct body, though termed in an honorary sense 'Extraordinary of the Guard'. They do not carry out any State functions, and are under the command of the Constable of the Tower alone. They are all retired soldiers. (The nickname 'Beef-eaters', which is sometimes associated with the Yeomen Warders, had its origin in 1669, when Count Cosimo, Grand Duke of Tuscany, was in England and, writing of 'this magnificent body of men', said: 'they are great eaters of beef, of which a very large ration is given them daily at the Court, and they might be called beef-eaters'.)

The Royal Company of Archers

The earliest written records of the Royal Company of Archers date from 1676. In 1704 a charter was granted to the Company by Queen Anne and the Royal Company still exists under that charter. During the royal visit to Edinburgh of King George IV in 1822, the Royal Company was made the King's Body Guard for Scotland.

The Royal Company's ceremonial duties include attendance on the Sovereign at Holyroodhouse. The Archers, in green uniforms and feathered bonnets and carrying bows, form a throne guard.

The Household Cavalry

The Household Cavalry comprises the Life Guards and the Blues and Royals (the latter regiment was created in 1969 by the amalgamation of the Royal Horse Guards [the Blues] and the Royal Dragoons). It provides a tank regiment and an armoured car regiment, with one mounted squadron from each regiment for State duties in London.

The Life Guards were created in 1660 just before the restoration of King Charles II when a mounted bodyguard was formed in Holland from royalists who had gone into exile with the King. The Royal Horse Guards had their origins in 1650 when Parliament ordered the raising of a horse regiment prior to Oliver Cromwell's second invasion of Scotland. The Royal Dragoons originated as a troop of horse raised by proclamation of King Charles II in 1661.

Normally one regiment is stationed overseas while the other is usually stationed at Windsor. Their State duties—the daily mounting of the Queen's Life Guard at Horse Guards, Whitehall, and escorts for the Queen on ceremonial occasions—are carried out by the two mounted squadrons stationed at Hyde Park Barracks. These squadrons are part of (and known as) the Household Cavalry Regiment (Mounted).

On occasions of State ceremonial the Colonels of both the Life Guards and the Blues and Royals carry out the office of *Goldstick*, created in 1678 because of public concern for the safety of King Charles II. It was ordered that one of the King's captains should attend on foot near him carrying an ebony staff or truncheon with a gold head engraved with the royal cypher and crown, and that another principal officer carrying an ebony staff with a silver head should wait near the captain and relieve him when necessary. Nowadays on ceremonial occasions the latter office, known as *Silverstick*, is performed by the Lieutenant-Colonel commanding the Household Cavalry.

The Foot Guards

The Foot Guards, like the Household Cavalry, are Household Troops and consist of five regiments: the Grenadier Guards, raised in 1656 from officers and men who had remained loyal to the royalist cause; the Coldstream Guards, originally formed by Cromwell from companies of the New Model Army, but later taking up arms in the service of the royalist cause and helping to restore the monarchy; the Scots Guards, re-formed in 1660 from a regiment raised in 1642 by the Marquis of Argyll; the Irish Guards, raised in 1900 at the instigation of Queen Victoria; and the Welsh Guards, raised by order of King George V in 1915.

The Foot Guards play a full part in active service overseas, but retain special duties at Court, regiments taking part in ceremonial events.

The Royal Arms, the Royal Standard and the Regalia

The Royal Arms

The first authentic English Royal Arms were borne by the Plantagenet kings in the twelfth century. The Queen's Arms (of which a simplified form is illustrated in this pamphlet) are in heraldic terms: quarterly, first and fourth gules, three lions passant guardant in pale, or (England); second, or, a lion rampant within a double tressure flory counterflory gules (Scotland); and third, azure, a harp or, stringed argent (Ireland); the whole encircled with the Garter.

Crown. A circle of gold, issuing therefrom four crosses patée and four fleurs-de-lis arranged alternately; from the crosses patée arise two golden arches ornamented with pearls, crossing at the top under a mound, surmounted by a cross patée, also gold, the whole enriched with precious stones. The cap is of crimson velvet, turned up ermine.

Crest. Upon the Royal helmet the crown proper, thereon statant guardant, or, a lion royally crowned also proper.

Supporters. On the dexter, a lion rampant guardant, or, crowned as the crest; and on the sinister, a unicorn argent-armed, crined, and unguled, or, gorged with a coronet composed of crosses patée and fleurs-de-lis, a chain affixed thereto passing between the fore-legs and reflexed over the back of the last.

Motto. Dieu et mon Droit.

The Royal Arms in Scotland

On the shield, the Arms of Scotland occupy the first and fourth quarters with those of England in the second quarter and Ireland in the third. The crest is a Scottish lion seated upon a throne and holding a sword and sceptre and the supporters are a unicorn on the right side and a lion on the left. The motto of Scotland—*In Defens*—is placed above the crest and the Garter is omitted.

The Royal Standard and the Union Flag

The Royal Standard or Royal Flag is the personal flag of the Sovereign and may be flown only when the Sovereign is actually present.

The British Union Flag, commonly known as the Union Jack, is the country's national flag. It is composed of the English cross of St George (a red cross on a white field), the Scottish cross of St Andrew (a diagonal white cross on a blue field) and the Irish cross of St Patrick (a diagonal red cross on a white field).

The Regalia

The regalia, or crown jewels, are the emblems of royalty and have held the same significance for the Kings and Queens of England for a thousand years. They symbolise the sense of continuity which the monarchy provides for the nation, and still have an important and valued place in the British heritage.

Since the coronation of King Charles II the regalia have been kept in the Tower of London under the guardianship of the Keeper of the Jewel House except when they are required for the coronation ceremony, in which they have a deep ritual significance. Most of the crown jewels on display at the Tower were made after the restoration of King Charles II in 1660, the previous regalia having been broken up and sold during the Republic of 1649–60. Two items which survived are the gilded silver Anointing Spoon and the gold Ampulla in the shape of an eagle, which holds the oil. In addition to the Imperial State Crown, with its thousands of precious stones, and to St Edward's Crown, with which the Sovereign is crowned, the other principal items of the regalia include the Jewelled State Sword and the Golden Spurs symbolising knightly chivalry, the Coronation Ring, the Golden Bracelets, the Golden Orb, surmounted by a jewelled cross signifying the Sovereign's obedience to the Christian faith, and the two sceptres; the Royal Sceptre with the Cross, which contains at the end of the golden bar the Star of Africa, the largest cut diamond in the world, and the Sceptre with the Dove—the first is a symbol of kingly power and justice, the second is one of equity and mercy.

The Scottish Regalia

The symbols of sovereignty in use when Scotland was a separate kingdom consist of the Crown, the Sceptre and the Sword of State, known as the Honours of Scotland. Associated with them are the Lord High Treasurer's mace and certain jewels bequeathed to King George III by Henry, Cardinal York. Unlike the royal ornaments of England, the Scottish regalia escaped destruction during the seventeenth century and are of great antiquity. The Crown dates from the sixteenth century or before—it was remodelled by order of King James V in 1540; the Sword of State was presented by Pope Julius II to King James IV in 1507; and the Sceptre was presented by Pope Alexander VI to King James IV in 1494. The Honours of Scotland, which are kept in the Crown Room at Edinburgh Castle, were carried to St Giles Cathedral on the occasion of the service held during the Queen's Coronation visit to Edinburgh in June 1953.

The Royal Yacht and the Queen's Flight

The Royal Yacht *Britannia*

The royal yacht *Britannia*, named and launched by the Queen at Clydebank (Scotland) in 1953, serves as an official and private residence for the Queen and other members of the royal family when they are engaged on visits overseas or are voyaging in home waters. The yacht also takes part in some naval exercises and undertakes routine hydrographic tasks while at sea. Designed to replace the 50-year-old *Victoria and Albert*, *Britannia* could be converted into a hospital ship in time of war.

Her gross tonnage is 5,769 tons (5,862 tonnes) and her continuous sea-going speed is 21 knots (10·8 metres per second). Refits and docking usually take place in the Royal Dockyard at Portsmouth.

The royal apartments are aft on the shelter deck and the royal staff accommodation is on the lower deck. The royal and state apartments contain some of the furniture from the *Victoria and Albert*. The Queen and the Duke of Edinburgh took a personal interest in the interior decorations, the choice of furnishings and the general fitting-out of the royal yacht.

The yacht is an independent command, administered personally by the Flag Officer Royal Yachts. He is normally appointed as an extra equerry to the Queen and, as such, is a member of the royal household. *Britannia*'s crew numbers 22 officers and 254 men when members of the royal family are embarked or when the vessel undertakes a long ocean voyage. Officers are normally appointed for two-year periods of duty. Two-thirds of the ratings are permanent crew members and remain attached to the ship for the rest of their service careers; the others are attached to the yacht for two-year periods only. They are all volunteers from the Royal Navy, but receive no special benefits in terms of pay, allowances or leave. Traditions of dress aboard the royal yacht include the wearing by seamen of naval uniform with the jumper inside the top of the trousers, which are finished at the back with a black silk bow. On all blue uniforms ratings wear white badges instead of the red which are customary in the Royal Navy. So far as possible orders on the upper deck are executed without spoken words or commands, and by long tradition the customary naval mark of respect of piping the side is normally paid only to the Queen.

The Queen's Flight

The Queen's Flight was created in 1936 (as the King's Flight) by King Edward VIII to provide air transport for the royal family's official duties. Based at Benson in Oxfordshire, the Flight is equipped with three twin-turboprop Hawker Siddeley *Andover* CC Mk 2 passenger transport aircraft and two Westland *Wessex* HCC 4 helicopters.

Provided by the Royal Air Force, the Flight operates under a general policy agreed between the Treasury and the Ministry of Defence. The Queen, the Queen Mother, the Duke of Edinburgh and the Prince of Wales are entitled to use it on all occasions. At the Queen's discretion it is also made available to other members of the royal family, but only on official duties. The Flight is used for official purposes by the Prime Minister and certain other people, such as senior ministers or visiting heads of State. The Ministry of Defence is responsible for all flights and routes of the aircraft of the Queen's Flight. The main cost of the Flight is borne upon defence votes.

Reading List

£

DAVIS, REGINALD. Elizabeth Our Queen. ISBN 0 00 211233 7.
	Collins	1976	4·95

DE SMITH, S. A. Constitutional and Administrative Law.
ISBN 0 14 080223 1. *Penguin* 1977 4·50

FISHER, GRAHAM *and* HEATHER. Monarchy and the Royal
Family. ISBN 0 7091 7814 X. *Robert Hale* 1979 8·50

FRASER, ANTONIA (*ed*). The Lives of the Kings and Queens of
England. ISBN 0 297 76911 1. *Weidenfeld & Nicolson* 1975 6·95

HIBBERT, CHRISTOPHER. The Court of St. James's.
ISBN 0 297 77631 2. *Weidenfeld & Nicolson* 1979 7·50

HOLDEN, ANTHONY. Charles, Prince of Wales.
ISBN 0 297 77662 2. *Weidenfeld & Nicolson* 1979 6·95

HOWARD, PHILIP. The British Monarchy in the Twentieth
Century. ISBN 0 241 89564 2. *Hamish Hamilton* 1977 7·50

LACEY, ROBERT. Majesty: Elizabeth II and the House of Windsor.
ISBN 0 09 128770 7. *Hutchinson* 1977 2·50

LONGFORD, ELIZABETH. The Royal House of Windsor.
ISBN 0 297 76829 8. *Weidenfeld & Nicolson* 1974 6·60

MONTGOMERY-MASSINGBERD, HUGH (*ed*). Burke's Guide
to the British Monarchy. ISBN 0 85011 024 5.
Burke's Peerage Limited in conjunction with New English Library 1977 8·50

NASH, ROY. Buckingham Palace. ISBN 0 354 04529 6
Macdonald Futura 1980 9·95

PAGET, JULIAN. The Pageantry of Britain.
ISBN 0 7181 1805 7. *Michael Joseph* 1979 9·95

PINCHES, J. H. *and* R. V. The Royal Heraldry of England.
ISBN 0 900455 25 X. *Heraldry Today* 1974 15·00

PLUMB, J. H. *and* WHELDON, HUW. Royal Heritage.
ISBN 0 563 17082 4. *BBC Publications* 1977 14·75

———— Royal Heritage—The Reign of Queen Elizabeth II.
ISBN 0 563 17862 0. *BBC Publications* 1981 10·50

TALBOT, GODFREY. The Royal Family. ISBN 0 600 37648 6.
Country Life 1981 10·00

VICKERS, HUGO. Debrett's Book of the Royal Wedding.
ISBN 0 905 64935 4. *Debrett's Peerage* 1981 8·95

83
451 3

Printed in England for Her Majesty's Stationery Office by Alpine Press, Watford
Dd. 716717 C100 6/81